William Kingston Sawyer

The Legend of Phyllis

With A Year of Song

William Kingston Sawyer

The Legend of Phyllis
With A Year of Song

ISBN/EAN: 9783337007065

Printed in Europe, USA, Canada, Australia, Japan

Cover: Foto ©Thomas Meinert / pixelio.de

More available books at **www.hansebooks.com**

THE LEGEND OF PHYLLIS

WITH

A YEAR OF SONG.

BY

WILLIAM SAWYER,

AUTHOR OF "TEN MILES FROM TOWN," ETC.

ILLUSTRATED BY JOHN PROCTOR.

TO

HENRY WILLETT Esq.,

OF

FINDON MANOR, SUSSEX,

IT IS THE AUTHOR'S PRIVILEGE

INSCRIBE THIS BOOK.

CONTENTS.

	PAGE
THE LEGEND OF PHYLLIS	1
EUDORIA	29

A YEAR OF SONG:

NEW YEAR NUMBERS	43
A MEETING	48
THE POET	53
THE TRIUMPH OF THE FLEUR-DE-LIS	55
ANGELICA	60
A PARTING	62
RAIN SONG	64
ANACREONTIC	67
CELADON	69
THE SINGERS	74
THE HOUR-GLASS	76
THE MISSAL	82

A YEAR OF SONG (*continued*):

	PAGE
SANDS OF THE SEA	84
TO EVA, WITH A SONG	89
THE GRANGE WINDOW	90
ROSE SONG	94
HOME AGAIN	96
THE PAGE	100
BARREN FAITH	104
HARALD'S WOOING	105
THE LETTER	110
LOVE SONG	113
THE FAMOUS STORY	115
A DREAM OF THE SEA	119
THE LORELEI	121
THE ASSASSIN	124
THERESE	125
MY LADY'S SECRET	129
A SUMMER DREAM	134
THE FIGHT FOR LIFE	136
VALLEY MEMORIES	143
CANONBURY PARK, MAY 30TH	145
THE TROOPER'S DEFENCE	146
ALLEGORY	150

A YEAR OF SONG (*continued*):

	PAGE
THE 'PRENTICE HOLIDAY	152
A LOST LOVE	157
A. T. M.	160
THE SPECTRE	162
THE WINDING OF THE SKEIN	165
IN A FRIEND'S POETICAL WORKS	17
THE LOST	172
THE DEAD OF THE YEAR	175
DURING THE TERROR	181
BLUE EYES FOR TRUTH	184
SONG OF AGE	187
BESIDE THE BROOK	189
THE BALLAD OF THREE	193
HOLLY TIME	195
THE HOLLY'S TEACHING	198

THE LEGEND OF PHYLLIS.

I

THE LEGEND OF PHYLLIS.

O, SOVRAN wonder of the Almond Tree,
That with the dawning hid itself in bloom
As, bare in rosy covert, hides a nymph!
Nor leaf had it, nor bud; but shuddered white,
Branching the moon. Now, see it, like a cloud
Red in the West; red to its blossom-heart
Of odorous beauty. Bright between the blooms
The sky of Spring is blue as loving eyes,
The wan gleams flicker—sunshine. On the air
Come wafted breaths of sweetness as from lips,
From parted lips of woman, and, with sweet,
Warm glows, the dainty shadows beauty casts
Lovingly fall. So flush with love and all

The charms of womanhood, the tree renews
The memory of the legend blent with it
Known to the wandering breeze, and in the song
The thrushes sing rehearsed from year to year.
That wondrous tale, in long forgotten days
A poet learned, and ever with sad brow
And heart that aching echoed of dead love,
Sung it from lips melodious of desire,—
A song of Phyllis and Demaphöon,
Of love defeating death.

     The siege was done,
Troy fallen, and among the Greeks came thence,
Long sailing, Theseus' son, Demaphöon,
His ship the rest outshining: white with sails
Of foam-drift, purple bordered, and its prow
The Minotaur, of his great father slain,
That golden-throated met the waves that round
Leapt flaming. Now, while yet the hindering seas
Held them from Athens, lo, the weary winds

Dropt, and three days they rocked in a great calm.
And on the fourth they saw where on the verge
Of the faint sea-line hovered—as a bird
Hovers in air—a fleck of snowy cloud,
Whereat great fear fell on the mariners.
And even as they reefed a flapping sail,
Touched by an instant puff of freshening wind,
The cloud grew, darkening as it grew, and borne
By the tempestuous forces whence it sprang,
Drew on toward them, gathering might, until
It filled the heavens—now a cloud, and now
What seemed to them the walls of Ilium
Risen anew, their battlemented heights
Flanked with great whorls of water—towers that grazed
The empyrean—bastioning ocean-walls
Impregnable, wide-curtained, masoned up
And ramparted with steeps of cloud and sea.
Onsweeping with the speed of winds it came,
And so the labouring ships o'ertook and charged

With shock of meeting seas, and thunderous crash.
Then straightway in its course it oversped
The fleet, in onward sweep, and rearing yet
Its airy towers, in lessening distance died.

Now, of the ships, some founder'd : some with gaps
Of yawning timbers righted : midst of all
The Minotaur, cumbered with riven sail
And trailing cordage—tackle of the ship—
Burned on the waves. The wind abating not
Harried what yet lived of the scattered fleet,
Till driven from their course, all reckoning lost,
They parted ship from ship and drifted wide
They knew not whither, through what unknown seas,
Or on what shores impending. But the Gods
Tenderly heedful of the Minotaur
Had of its souls compassion ; not in vain
Entreated of Demaphöon, himself

Celestial of descent, for Theseus' birth,
Brought Neptune joy, and, in their sorest need,
Rendered them up in safety to the land.

A long tongue of the barren Thracian coast
Sterile with tamarisk growth and arid grass,
Received them from the insatiable seas.
There all in vain temple they sought or tomb,
In-running cave or green leaf-sheltering tree :
Nor looked they upon human face, nor found
Aught meet for food, as bird, or nested egg,
Or ripening berry, nor could any hear
The ripple of sweet waters in the grass.
A weary night they hungered there : but morn
Beheld them clamorous ; of Demaphöon
Beseeching help and succour, since, remote
A swan's flight only from the shore—or so
They reckoned it—there dwelt the Queen o' the land,
Lycurgus' daughter, Phyllis ; suit to her

From Theseus' son must save them, then what course
But to her walls to hasten presently?
To this he hearkened doubting, yet constrained
Of faces wan with fasting and fierce eyes,
He gathered from his people whom he might,
Scant retinue, and inward from the shore
Wended he knew not whither. But ere night
They drew toward a city, and in midst
Beheld a palace reared, pavilioned domes,
Begirt with twinkling minarets that flashed
Smit with the sunset. Now, ere they drew near,
The bruit of all that had befallen them
Had reached the ears of Phyllis, and she thought,
"A Queen's son craving succour of a Queen
Were sight unmeet and base in sovereignty,
Befits we greet him coming, as the Gods
Were gracious in their favour and had sought
To honour us in this most honoured guest,
And proffer him of all things ere he ask."

So, knowing of her maidens when he came,
She in her queenly splendour girt about
Went forth to meet him. And Demaphöon
Uplifting eyes beheld her as she moved,
Regal, with scintillant glint and interglow
Of blending gems. Wound gold about her brow,
The gold of gathered tresses woven fair,
Glittered for diadem. Around her feet
Wide as a wave, a robe of shimmering sweep,
Purple and gold inwoven, thread for thread,
Sparkled its shining way. Enmeshed in light,
Her bosom netted in a diamond net
Shone pearl-wise, and for girdle, glittering
With gems through all its undulant length, a snake
Of triple coil circled her waist and lolled
A heavy head with onyx aspic eyes.
So moved she lustrous, gleaming in the sun,
In the snatched moment of the absolute prime
Of beauty, blossom-brief, and in the touch
Of its own ripe perfection perishing:

So glorious drew she near Demaphöon
Who, unregardful of aught else, beheld
Her face, and looking in her face, saw youth,
And beauty shining in the light of youth,
And seeing loved.

                She, too, beholding him
A Prince that sprung from the Immortals, bore
Their aspect,—youth in manhood glorified,—
Crimsoned, a lily damask'd to the core:
And hungered for the music of his voice.
Somewhat he murmured faintly, and his words,
In cadenced ripples, rippled to her heart:
Her eyes forewent their queenly gaze and drooped,
As curious of the mosses at his feet,
Yet sidelong marked a brow, that wide and white,
Locks over - clustered ; marked the light that brimmed
Deep-caverned eyes; the passion-parted lips;
The heroic frame compactly squared,

Deep-chested, supple, tapering from the girth,
To rosy knee and foot of curve supreme
That arched the untrod anemone.

                                        Few words
Of gracious welcome, grateful homage, served
Where heart for heart interpreted. Their hands
Met burning. Somewhat murmured she, or meant,
Of honour by the Gods accorded her,
In Theseus' son, welcome for Theseus' self,
As equal hero, with like honied words
Befitting courtly wont. Then, of her grace
And of her boundless bounty she, straightway,
Bestowed her palace of the hundred gates,
Of jasper, purple-shadowed, on the Prince,
And on his people for their sojourning,
And so departed, as from out her fane
A Goddess flashes.

                      Wondrous was the place
And fair, for therein all the arts of Thrace

Contended, and its walls the spoils of war
Made glorious. And therein Demaphöon
And all his folk abode in festival,
Lacking no tending, and the meanest ate
The meat of kings. And every morrow came
The Queen, and in her coming brought delight
And, to the Princely heart that loved her, brought
Rapture tumultuous as the gleamy clash
Of smitten cymbals. Joyful were these twain
With joy of all things fed,—the breeze of morn,
The freshness of the freshening Spring, the blue
Of April skies, the hues of bud and bloom,
The breath of flowers: all things that breathe and
  bring
Joy to the world, to them love's raptures brought.

So day was heaped on day as flower on flower,
And night with night mingled in starry round,
And in the rapturous holding of a dream
Tarried Demaphöon, for life to him

Was Phyllis ; duty Phyllis ; Theseus,
Companions of the war, and friends who dwelt
Remote in Athens, nothing,—Phyllis all.

But now grew on the season of clipt days
And fiery sunsets, of fierce winds that chase
The clouds, and rend the forest, and ride hard
The mad sea-coursers by their frothy manes.
And, for they feared the wintry seas, or felt
The quickening of home-memories in their hearts,
His folk began to urge Demaphöon
With promptings of return.   A little while
He silenced them ; but evermore they broke
Into complainings, murmurous, until
He dared not hold them longer. Then he sought
Where Phyllis, steeped in noonday languors rose,
And spake, and from his clasping hands she slid,
And lay in a long swoon upon the earth,
And thereby held him for a space ; but soon
The murmuring rose again and yet again,

And he, what could he but rehearse anew
The hateful truth; she heard but spake no word,
Only went shuddering ghost-like from his gaze,
And hid herself within her palace walls
As in a tomb.   Yet there Demaphöon
Sought her, and showed her all his agony.
His heart-throes and the anguish of the strife
'Twixt love that clung and duty that forbade
A longer stay; so prayed her pity him,
Distraught at parting yet constrained to part.
Too long his love had held him, all too long
For glory and for manhood; it behoved
He sailed thenceforth for Athens; but he sware
The sickle moon above them should not round
To light him shoreward ere he came again.
That oath upon the altar of her breast
He sware, and sealed it on her lips.   Thereat
All woman, she for answer wept; but when
Against his will her silent tears prevailed
As little as the foamy spray the rock

O'ermasters, all the Queen in her revived.
It was Lycurgus' daughter, regal yet
Even in her sorrows, and constrained to wield
The sceptre o'er herself as o'er her realms,
Strained rosy palms to heaven and prayed the Gods
So succour Theseus' son or so avenge
His perfidy as he should keep or break
The promise of his lips. This done she waved
A hasty hand and charged him brokenly
Depart her shores. Sad was Demaphöon,
Heart-sick and sad; the rest with fierce delight
Beheld again the Minotaur, enriched
With store of all things to make glad the voyage,—
For so the Queen had willed,—and resting not,
As men with the new wine of hope grown glad,
All eagerly made ready to be gone.

The moon was rising redder than the sun
Through the flushed eve, and by its lurid gleam
The hapless Phyllis stood beside the ship,

Strained to the leaping heart of him she loved,—
A wraith, arm-circled to a human breast,—
And as it rose and whitened o'er the sea,
And glimmer'd on their meeting faces white,
The severing word was said, and with its sound
As from a shell's lips softly murmurous,
They lingered out one long embrace—the last!
Then the waves sundered them. The argent round
Of the great ocean broadened to the gaze
Of the lone Queen, until its smooth expanse
Glittered immeasurable. Swift of flight
The ship sped, curving to the breeze; and while
The snowy sails blackened against the moon,
Drove to the sea-line, and through tears that
    blurred
Distorting all on which they looked, and filled
With anguish sea and sky, died from her sight.

Thence day was flung on day as weed on weed,
And night on night heaping made dark the world

To Phyllis, and as from her eyes had fled
The ships, so fled belief in Theseus' son
Out of her hungering heart. Watching she saw
The rounding and the wrecking of the moon
That was to light him back to her, and saw
Strange moons that waxed and waned and were as
    lights,
Burning above the corse of her dead hope.
Long weary days and ever weary nights
She paced the barren shores, the barren sands,
Low lying in the ooze : face wan, eyes red,
A bine of passion-flowers round a brow
Warm from spilt roses; paced with wringing hands
Hard clasping and with ever restless feet.
And ever doubt wrestled with doubt and oft
Had conquered, in sick brain and weary heart,
But that her lips repeating what her love
Made music, comforted, and kept her sane.
Aloud to the still night and to the winds,
That swirled the loosened shock of sun-bright hair

About her as she wandered, thus she sang:

"Thou art not false, not false, Demaphöon,
To me or to thy heart, not false, not false!
The ships are foundered in the weltering seas,
Great winds have rent them; thy white limbs are sleeked
Of wondering Naiads in sea-sunken caves,
Or thou art held of monsters, or art slain,
In thine own land of thine own people slain;
My eyes will not behold thee any more,
But false thou art not, false to love and me!

"I gave thee to the winds and seas and urged
Thy going hence, thy swift return; thy vows
Rang on my true heart true: they live for me
Warm as the living touch of hand in hand.
Men whisper me of Theseus' treachery
To Ariadne; bid me note that blood
Is strong in kind, false father, falser son.

I hear but heed not, knowing thou art dead,
Or if life hold in thee thou wilt return,
Thou art not false to love, not false to me!

" Thou livest not, O loved Demaphöon,
In vain I pace the shore and rend the day
And rend the night with anguish; all in vain
I watch the sails that thicken as the winds
Blow shoreward, but there comes not sail of thine.
The stately prows drive hither, hither drives
No more the golden Minotaur that smit
The spraying waves to flame; I watch in vain,
I shall not look upon thee any more,
But as in life beloved so in death,
I know thee true to love and true to me."

Time went, and winter whitened all the land,
Blank to the heart of her who waited still
For him who came not; held him dead and yet
Looked ever for his coming. To the winds

And to the waves she murmured evermore,
Still paced the shore and pacing saw the ship—
Or deemed she saw it—in the offing, shrieked,
Waved arms exultant, burst into the surf
To reach it, then beheld the tacking sails
Veering for other havens and so swooned.
Or, phrenzied, in the sunset splendours saw,
Mid amaranth-dropping clouds, Demaphöon,—
His face a glory, and his out-blown locks,
With the sea-sparkle on them,—onward borne,
With limbs effulgent, robe of rainbow gleams
Wide to the wind, and sandals diamonded,—
Imperial of presence as a God!
Thus, lured toward a passing ship, or moved
By such a frenzy, on a day when none
Gave heed, she waded from the shore, and fell
Face downward in the frothing of the sea,
And in the scooping shingle sank, and caught
In the strong net of a receding wave,
Strove helpless in the shrieking drag of it,

And overmastered in contention--died!

On the long tongue of black low-lying land
Deep in the ooze, they buried her, that so
The winds might blow about her with a sound
Of flapping sails, and the waves comfort her
With music as of swift in-running keels.
Two days her people mourned her, on the third,
Coming while yet a mist on sea and shore
Hung dense and dyed with saffron of the morn,
They sought her grave, but where they looked
    for it
Found antler'd branches spectral in the mist,
And with stretched hands grasped not the air, but
    held
Fair branches lithe and wet with rime, and knew
That in the night from out the grave a tree
Had risen with the girth and growth of years!
Now, while they questioned, doubting of this thing,
A corner of the mist blew wide, a gleam

Of morning smit the tree, and in the light
The rimy branches tremulous with gems
Swayed glittering, and with every querulous breeze
Their diamond sparkles rained upon the grave.

Great joy was in their hearts who looked on this,
And knew it of the Gods. And now the morn
Freshened, and slowly from the barren sea
And barren land the mist rose fold on fold,
And the wan sun looked out on a wan world;
Then as the eyes of their dead queen had sought,
Each weary morn, the glimmering hyaline
Of the wide ocean freshening in the light,
So, they who mourned for love of her, strained eyes
Over the ocean, shining silver-smooth,
Save where the wind-caught waters rippled white,
For any hope. And, lo, across the waste,
Far in the east, there drove the glimmering fleet,

Led by the ship that bore Demaphöon,
Its white sails purple bordered, and the waves
About the Minotaur as licking flames.
Swiftly the ships blew landward, swiftest his
Who bent above the monster of the prow,
And so drew in toward the yeasty surf,
And, waiting a great wave, upon its rise
Rode lightly in.   Demaphöon was first
To leap into the surf and wade, and there,
While yet they looked on him as on a wraith,
Stood questioning in their midst.   What thing was
    this?
What marvel and what portent?   And their Queen
Not in their midst, and wherefore?   "She is dead,"
They answered, and he echoed, "Dead!" and still
"Dead!" with his white, incredulous face all
    changed
And like a mask.   "Phyllis is dead!"   Here then
They told what had befallen: of the love
That, a dividing sword, drove to the heart

Of her they mourned, and of the grief that slew
    her;
Nor stinted of the wonder of the night,
That in its strangeness had usurped their grief;
But showed him all.

                Their words Demaphöon
Heard, but as one that swooning hears a voice
Far off; from whom the world slips while the day
Darkens, and hearing, fell upon the earth,
And grovelled weeping; lay his length and wept
And moaned as men die moaning. Through long
    hours
Outstretch'd he lay and silent: heeding nought
In the dumb heart-break of his agony.
Then, as of its excess defeated, ebbed
The brimming passion of his grief, he drew
Toward the tree; threw arms about its girth,
And clasped and kissed the silver rind, and prest
A smooth girl-cheek against it, murmuring,

And, as dead ears had hearing, cried aloud,
Cried to his lost love, lost within the grave :—

" O, Phyllis, O my love, if thou perchance
Canst hear me—pitied of the pitying Gods
That give but cannot spare,—lo where I kneel!
I keep my great oath sworn upon thy heart
To love thee, to return to thee ; I come
Through hungering seas and perils manifold,
To claim thee of thyself, so vowed to me
As never in all time was woman vowed.
From thy lone grave wherein thou liest, slain
Of thy great love, behold me! Thine in life,
Thine only, and in death, as life, thine own.

" O Phyllis, if indeed dead ears may list
The wail of dying lips, give heed, give heed !
Thy soul had faith in all things and in all.
The day went from thee, and thou didst not fear
The day's return : the night died with its stars,

Slain of the dawn, and thou didst not despair;
The seas ebbed from thy feet, thou all content;
The summer went, 'It will come back,' thou saidst.
Yet trusting all things, me thou couldst not trust;
I true to thee as day, night, stars, and seas,
As flower time and as fruit time; as the course
Of the recurrent seasons, found no faith,
Orbed in thy love, yet true to thee in vain.

"O Phyllis! O my lost, my lost! The blooms
Of passion lightly rooted swiftly die,
Lacking the nurture of the steadfast heart;
But thou, sole centred in thy true love's troth,
Couldst, loving, doubt, and yet not doubting live,
But gav'st thy doubt up to resolving death.
Brave heart! true heart! I have no scorn for thee.
My grief shall cast no shadow on thy grave
Made sacred of the Gods. I do but mourn

Thy virgin life snapt in its lily-prime,
Thy beauty's light stamped out, and earth henceforth
Dark to my stumbling feet. I can but weep
And weary Love that glorified our lives
With Iris' splendours—blossoms of sown tears—
Till Her dread function he shall seize, and give
My spirit wing to flutter back to thee."

So mourning wasted love and broken life,
All sorrowful, he clung about the tree,
And kneeling claspt and fondled it, and wept
A boy's hot passion of burning, blinding tears.
And as he knelt thus, lo! a miracle!
The human heart that stirred within the sap
Quickened with love as at the touch of Spring,
Auroral flushes panted through the tree;
A warming glow suffused it; with a pulse
Of ardent heat, flame-hearted blossoms sleeked
Its branches, rosy-smooth and with a haze

Of summer noons upon them. Warm with life
The blossoms claspt his brow and clustering lay
Upon his cheek, and to his lips were lips
That throbbed to kissing and his amorous breath
Met with ambrosial odours. This was love's
Response to love. The pitying Eros this
Accorded, and in memory thereof
Throughout the winters of all after years
The almond blossoms come before the leaves.

EUDORIA.

LUDORIA.

I am the woman of the witch's eyes,
That looked men into sin.

My beauty was a snare;
My red lips slew.
My rounded breast,
Heaving, moon-white, rent hearts
As the great orb rends with unrest the waves
That stiffen up
In a fierce clutch for her,
And swoon and drop
Foaming upon the sands.

I had no mercy; no!
I made a net for men—
A wide, great net—
Of my hair, ankle-long,
And bluer, blacker than the grapes I tore
From the bronze vines
To twist up with its lengths.
No mercy; none!
My voice
Had the shell's murmur,
Treacherously sweet;
With soft insidious pulsings, interknit
With memories and promptings and desires;
Its dulcet whispers toying with the chords
That quicken passion.
Music absolute;
Music, yet happier he
Who hears, and hearing shudders at the shriek
Of the torn mandrake.

So beautiful, so merciless—
And now !
Look on me. See ! My face
Is a dead face.
The red of autumn sunsets in my cheek
And on my lips—
My fierce, hot lips—
Has all burnt out.
I am as white as ashes on the hearth,
Wan as a wraith ;
Out of great caverns now
My witch-eyes glare,
And men are scared at them, and women
    swoon.
Look ! see !
My golden armlets hang
Loose on this bone, my arm.
My arm !
Is this the rounded snow that I have kissed
And fondled with a hand as rosy-soft

As almond-blossom ?
God ! my poor, thin hand !

What ails me ?
What is that of which we ail—
We women—
When, like a robe,
Our beauty slips from us, and all our youth
Goes in a night ?
Not love :
That is delight—
Rose-hearted, languorous love
Is keen delight,
Not steel-sharp pain,
Dull agony,
A lifting of red lids from aching eyes
That look on a dead world.

Not love.   Ah, no
Our hearts hold love

As a cup wine;
A cup Cellini has wrought
And crusted over with gems.
What if hot riot fire
The blood of the purple draught,
Does the cup throb?
Do the jewels quiver and shoot,
Or Cellini's bacchanals leap
At the feel of the flame within?

It was not love.
I had not looked on men,
Seen them rise from my feet,
Stagger, and reel, and go
Ghost-white,
To fall, a wren in a net,
To crouch, a hound at his feet,
Watching his bloodshot eyes
Or the lift of his chiding hand.
I loathed him in the moment that we met.

Swart and brute,
The Dacian surf of the frieze,
What should he out of the phalanx? Slave, most
    fit
To tug at a wheel in a triumph of Roman fools.
His words
Struck on my ears like blows;
Struck on my ears and still
Through my numb brain
They surge and sing.
As he looked out
Under his low, wide brow,
His iron brow
Ploughed with its ruts,
His eyes quenched mine.
They were molten, I think, or flame;
But a mist obscured my own,
I could only weakly gaze
At the dusky Dacian face,
At the square jaw,

And the cruel curve of a mouth
To lie with, to curse with, never
To shape to a tender thought.

My breast was flint.
God, that a slave like this
Should have struck out its fire—
That look of his should lift
My creeping hair,
Or word from those hard lips
Drive ice into my veins!
I hated him;
Hated myself the more.
Yet when he went,
Frenzy was in my blood,
My throat dust-dry,
My eye-balls fire;
Unutterable throes
Dragged me I knew not where.
Into the night,

Through the wet trees
I stole, to watch the way that he had gone,
To listen to his step,
Loud, loud to me,
Though he had waded the long meadow-grass;
Loud to my ear that heard
The dead leaf drop,
The bird stir in the nest,
And the spider, as he swung,
Plumb with prismatic line
The darkness under the bough.
I loathed him as I stood
Bareheaded to the dews,
The moonlight spilt
Upon my head,
Here where my hair is white,
Age-white,
Not shimmering with the gloss
As where the lamplight falls
On the blue-black coils below.

Hatred was in my heart,
Hatred, or what
Stronger than hate,
Fiercer than passion
Subtler than desire,
Curdles the creeping blood, and renders up
To frenzy all the avenues of life?

Long hours I stood
Grinding hot temples into icy palms
That claspt but cooled not.
Lone as the night,
Lone as the leper moon,
Outcast of God,
Abandoned of His stars
That shrink from her
And shudder at the horror of her face!
My doom had come
Swift as the lightning flash,
That fierce and keen,

Stabs to its purpling heart the Autumn night.
The knell of joy
Had sounded through my years,
My stricken years, as sounds
The bell that ends the Carnival.
The whirl,
The eddying coil
Tumultuous riot, dissolute mirth,
And then,
As the dull boom from the great Minster stops,
Cessation—silence—
Death !

A YEAR OF SONG.

NEW YEAR NUMBERS.

Trust Him that is thy God, and have no fear:
His eyelids ache not with the drowse of sleep,
He cannot tire, and how should He forget?

Self-centred in His own eternity,
He that is All is cause and law of all;
Alike in orb and atom infinite.

The worlds He soweth broadcast with His hand,
As o'er the glebe the sower soweth seed,
Till with His glory all the heavens are sown.

Yet perfect from His shaping fingers sent
The rain-drop glitters populous with life;
And in a jewelled surcoat wheels the gnat.

Behold the yearly miracle of Spring!
The pinky nipples of the budding leaves
Break in a night, and lo, the wood is green!

Art thou more bare than is the winter wood,
Or less esteemed of Him who gives thee joy
In the first rustle of the April leaves?

And if thy prime be gone and thou lament,
"The leaves are falling and the fruit is done!"
Yet shrink not from the winter of thy days.

See where the cruel winds have swept the trees
And all are branching bare against the night,
There, in the barren spaces, hang the stars.

So when the leafage of thy days is past,
And life is desolate, repine thou not,—
God can give thee the stars of heaven for fruit!

Nor fear thou death. God's law is gain in loss:
Growth and decay obey a common law,
The starry blossom and the seed are one.

Think! Thou wert born and fashioned for a world
Assorted to thy needs and thy delights,
And wherein thou hast dwelt and had content.

Not of thy strength nor cunning didst thou come,
Into the fief and heritage of life;
And shall all fail thee in thy going hence?

Thou art not of thyself a thing alone,
But of the earth which shaped and nourisheth
And is thy vital warmth and fount of life.

Its mountains are thy brothers, and its woods,
Its seas have lent thee, and its affluent winds
Spare thee thy being for a little space.

All things have part in thee as thou in all
Hast thine own part; thy soul its part in God,
And all enduring, shalt not thou endure?

The salt foam of the sea upon thy lips,
The blown sand of the desert in thy face,
Shall these outlast the ages and not thou?

The star shines and the cloud slips from its face
Each to its function, moving to one law;
And both imperishable, cloud and star.

Content thyself and comfort thee in this;
In God's design is neither best nor worst,
To Him the greater is not nor the less.

The All of all embraces gain and loss,
His steadfast and His fleeting are as one,
And of His ordered change is ordered good.

In Him love bounds the infinite of might,
And He who giveth both to live and die
Is equal Lord of Life and Lord of Death.

A MEETING.

No leaves as yet, but on the trees
   A tender flush of green,
And, black in many a fork and branch,
   The last year's nests were seen:
Bare half the boughs; the stems were bare
   Save where around them grown,
The shining ivy-tangle wrought
   A verdure not their own.

The early violets were out,
   Their wafted fragrance blent
With acrid taint of trodden leaves,
   As through the wood I went;

The hidden nooks the primrose lit,
  The snowdrop pure and cold,
And in the clefts the crocus shot
  In points of living gold.

Deep down into the wood I went,
  The birds sang overhead—
The thrush sang there a month ago,
  Else all the wood was dead;
Now every bird was back, and each
  Had in my joy a part;
The happy birds sang on, and I
  Went singing in my heart.

The dewy freshness of the dawn
  Sparkled on all around;
My step was lighter than a boy's,
  My footfall made no sound;

With eager, flaming eyes I went
    Seeking a face that, fair
And fresh, was hidden from my gaze
    But to my heart was there.

"The eyes deceive, the heart is true,"
    This thought was in my breast,
"Love would discern her were she hid
    Close in a leafy nest;
If this were June and all the wood
    Stood dense with swathing green,
She would be present to my love,
    Detected though unseen."

Throbbing delight in every vein,
    Pulses that burn and thrill,
For ecstacy I could have swooned;
    My listening heart stood still;

Then onward with a joyous cry
    And quickened step I sped,—
Between the trees, before my eyes
    A ribbon fluttered red !

THE POET.

The poet and the prophet yet are one
   As when their brows with equal bays
   Were girt, in dim remembered days;
Other prophetic utterance Fate has none.

No inspiration is there save of earth;
   Who seeth much he seeth far,
   Within his ken God's counsels are,
For in the present has the future birth.

But wherefore should the laurel clasp his brow
   Whose brain to rhythmic frenzy wrought
   Confuses ecstacy with thought,—
Mocked by the rustle of Dodona's boughs?

Or his who holds,—defeated of desire,—
    The subtle sweets of sense divine,—
    Love's roses in the drench of wine,
Their burning petals loosening, fire in fire.

How should his mouth with sacred fervour glow
    Whose songs the heat of Venus fan,—
    The Venus pitiless to man,
Pandemos, nourisher of sin and woe?

Or his, who lightly girding him for song,
    Tyrtæus of each little cause,
    From jarring factions seeks applause,
And clamours for the right or for the wrong?

Weaker than weakest wave upon the shore
    These snatch in vain the ringing lyre;
    Vainly in ecstacy expire :—
Libations to Cassandra let them pour.

True sons are they of her whose frothy lip,
  Yet with prophetic fervour white,
  The equal Lord of song and light
Touched with his sacred tongue's extremest tip;

Touched, and she knew not, and none hearing knew
  Whether in foamy mutterings broke
  Counsels oracular, or spoke
A babbling tongue, confounding false and true.

THE TRIUMPH OF THE FLEUR-DE-LIS.

The moon was red, and wide of girth
Orbed a span above the earth;
Lapp'd in light the meadow lay,
   Yet the grasses were not green;
For the light was not as the light of day,
   They glowed in ruddy sheen;
Mystic was that April night,
And it saw a wondrous sight,
Beautiful as sight may be—
The Triumph of the Fleur-de-lis.

By the level brook that glowed
Greenly golden as it flowed,

Moved the Pageant, strangely shown
To a music of its own.
Out of sleep the meadow broke,
And the meadow daisies woke,
Opened wide their owl-round eyes,
Gazed, ray-lidded with surprise ;
Violets started from the deeps
Of their happy, odorous sleeps ;
Maiden lilies whitely rose
Troubled from their pure repose ;
Shining grasses, flags in sheaves,
   Mosses greening as they grow ;
   All that shares to overflow
In the joy of budding leaves,
In the gladness of the Spring,
Stirred to sudden wondering !

First, in doublets hued of flame,
   Of gold and crimson blending bright,
On the trumpeter Tulips came,

THE TRIUMPH OF THE FLEUR-DE-LIS.

Blowing shrill, as blow they might,
Martial music through the night.

Then the Ferns by many a score
The fronds, their pennons, bore,
Every frond a swelling sail
Straining broad against the gale.

Flamen Wall-flowers, as they pass'd,
   Burning censers softly swung,
   And the subtle incense flung
To the air its sweetness cast.

Then, in pomp of festival,
Came the pride and crown of all.
Girt about with sedgy glaives,
   The Fleur-de-lis, in long array,
Moved imperial midst their slaves,
   Moved on their triumphal way;

Guarding well, yet to the night
Half revealing—light in light—
Ne'er beheld of mortal eyes,
The mystic signs that symbolise
The three-fold sacredness which sheds
Its halo round anointed heads;
While above their state unfurled,
The purple banners flapped and curled.

Still the pageant onward wore;
   Fitly ordered, winding far,
Stately Jonquils meetly bore
   Each its glimmering star;
Hyacinths with locks unwrought
From the netted braid, and caught
   By the intertangling breeze;
   And, as shining Nymphs, with these
Daffodils, and o'er the rest
   The cressets of the Marigold,
   Redly flamed, as each might hold
The wonder of the phœnix' nest.

Nor were lacking, whitely dim,
The tender flowers named of him
   Who, stricken of his beauty, died,
Nor a hundred phantoms more,
   Virgin-vested, crimsoned, pied,
   Which, in passing glorified,
Blossom-pennons bore.

Thus the bright procession sped
   Till the ruddy moon, that dipt
   Earthward, on a sudden slipt
Out of heaven, and in the dead
Of darkness all the marvel fled.

ANGELICA.

Fair is my love, so fair,
   I shudder with the sense
Of what a light the world would lose
   Could she go hence.

Sweet is my love, so sweet,
   The leaves that, fold on fold,
Swathe up the odours of the rose,
   Less sweetness hold.

True is my love, so true;
   Her heart is mine alone,
The music of its rhythmic beat
   Throbs through my own.

Dear is my love, so dear,
    If I but hear her name,
My eyes with tears of rapture swim,
    My cheek is flame.

Spare her, Immortals, spare,
    Till all our days are done—
Your heaven is full of angel forms,
    Mine holds but one.

A PARTING.

Come, let us take hands together
    As when, summers ago, we stood
In the haze of the sultry weather
    In the heart of the little wood.

No! we never again shall linger,
    Never moments like those beguile,
Yielding slowly, finger to finger,—
    Yet tightening our grasp the while!

'Twas the heart's first rapture of passion,
    A transport that has no name,
Predestined to swift cessation,
    When the ashes should choke the flame.

Life grew bright, as the wood will brighten
   In rosily deepening eves;
Grew cold, as when dewily whiten
   The smooth of its moon-litten leaves.

There are times for loving and leaving,
   There are seasons of the heart,
And parting is better than cleaving,
   When 'tis harder to meet than part.

And in love there is no renewing;
   Life never can know again
The bliss that gives rapture to wooing,
   Though farther from pleasure than pain.

Still let us take hands together
   As we did in the hours we stood,
In the haze of the heat of the weather,
   In the heart of the little wood.

RAIN SONG.

Is the rain sad ? Ah, no !
    Not the dear April rain,
    The sweet, white rain :
These are glad tears that flow,
    Not tears of pain.

Through the blue heavens take
    The clouds their bird-swift way,
    Their white, pure way :
The clouds that part and break,
    In diamond spray.

RAIN SONG.

The clouds that die in showers,
    Hues of the rainbow give,
    Its beauty give,
That in its dyes the flowers
    May brightly live.

Faint odours of the Spring,
    The subtle breath of fields,
    Of grass in fields,
Scents that to mosses cling,
    The sweet rain yields.

The song of its delight,
    To the warm noon it sings,
    Tenderly sings;
And to the quiet night
    Its music brings,

All happy things rejoice
 In the bright April rain,
 The freshening rain ;
Exulting that its voice
 Is heard again.

ANACREONTIC.

To love and in excess of loving lose,
This is the lot of all things and of all,
For ever love's extreme is love's defeat.

The sky that held the one white cloud of noon
And warmed it in its bosom, lost it so
In rainbow flushes and in diamond rain.

The air that loved the flame and fondled it
And fed it into beauty with itself
Quenched out its life with over cherishing.

The flame that saw the water beautiful
And sought to clasp it to its fervid heart
Held, as Ixion held his love, a cloud!

So love is ever slain of love,—and thou,
Wilt thou too pass away and be to me,
To me who love, a memory and tears?

CELADON.

Our Celadon? He of the apple cheek
   And soft, girl eyes? The story is soon told.
He loved the Marquise with the radiant hair
   Bright with that moonlight tint of virgin gold,
Pined for the cheek that glowed, as to its lips
   With warming bloom the honeysuckle glows,
And languished for her blue eyes' violet depths,
   And mouth rose-sweet and redder than the rose.

It was before the greening of the wood
   Slowly from leafy bud to leafy bloom,
Had darkened all its glowing heart of light
   And made therein a purple heart of gloom;

While yet the sunshine wholly makes the morn,
    While yet the trailing clouds no shadows fling,
The violet time, when days are bright and brief
    And mated finches in their nesting sing.

The raging west had flamed itself to dust
    And throbbed in dying embers, as he lay
Beyond the satin smoothings of her robe;
    His face a ghost's, and yet his laugh was gay.
She did not mark the trouble in his eyes,
    Or how he stifled agony in jest;
But she was quick to note when, as he rose,
    There fell a crumpled letter from his breast?

She saw it, and she saw the furtive snatch
    That followed. "Do you bring me a surprise—
A poem—lucent verse?" He closed his hand:
    And made to hide the letter from her eyes!

"Nothing—'tis nothing." "Show it me," she cried;
 "I do not doubt, but—" Forth a hand she thrust.
"I cannot." "No? And wherefore?" "Let us say,
 Because in love trust merits equal trust."

Her bitten lip shot out. "Trust merits trust,
 But I may not be trusted? Is it so?"
"To-morrow, if I live or die," he said:
 But she rose up in scorn and bade him go!
"And if to-morrow serve, why not to-night?
 You dare not show it me!" He did not speak,
But gazed at her dismayed, and groaned, and went,—
 Nor saw her, reeling, swoon with stifled shriek.

All wearily dragged out the April night,
 Till the low clouds let in a sullen dawn:
All wearily the Marquise watched till cries
 Mingled with heavy footsteps on the lawn;

Then darting to her window saw where men
    Trampled her flowers and Celadon they bore,
Rigid, with starting eyes, but, in the clutch
    Of his dead hand, the letter red with gore.

That showed her all. Showed that a sneering lip
    Had made a salon merry with her name,
Till Celadon had scored the slanderer's face
    With a red welt,—and so a challenge came.
That letter held it! He had known his fate,
    Known there had come an end of love and youth,
Yet had lain there and jested at her feet,
    And made her merry and withheld the truth!

"For if I live," he thought, "she will not grieve;
    And if I die, too soon her tears will flow;
And it were shame a man's last hours were spent
    In torturing a loving heart with woe."

So, calmly, he went forth to meet his fate ;
 Bearing the pang of her mistrust he went.
It had been his—brave heart !—to clear her name
 And spare her tears,—and he was all content.

THE SINGERS.

CHERRY-BLOSSOM nested
    Sweet the thrushes sing;
Thrushes freckle-breasted
    Lifting heart and wing;
For joy of cherry-blossoms evermore they sing.

Comes the time of berries
    They will sing no more;
Hiding among cherries,
    Happy in their store;
In the time of cherries thrushes sing no more.

THE SINGERS.

  Thus, O Poet, singing
    In thine own delight ;
  Ecstacy upspringing
    Tunes thy lips aright,
Evermore to music shaping thy delight.

  Even while thou starvest
    All thy heart is song ;
  After comes the harvest,
    Comes thy fame ere long ;
But the hours of fulness are not hours of song.

THE HOUR-GLASS.

The sea-green moonlight fills the cell
   Wherein, at midnight, prays alone
A kneeling brother, lank and lean,
   And still as carven out of stone.

High, where the three-feet wall is pierced,
   Against a lancet-window, leaps,
Swinging in gusts, a vine,—and near
   A squinting gargoyle grimly peeps.

Before the image of our Lord
   A pictured missal open lies,
Its wrought initials, burnish'd gold,
   Its columned words in blending dyes.

THE HOUR-GLASS.

Beside the book, an hour-glass set,
    Half in its oaken frame conceals
Two shining bubbles, lightly blown,
    Through which the sand-thread redly steals.

Not on the image of the Lord,
    Not on the missal's dazzling blaze;
But on the red sand's wasting thread
    The kneeling brother bends his gaze.

To turn that glass from hour to hour,
    Throughout the day, throughout the night,
He makes the duty of a life
    Which Heaven, he deems, has shaped aright.

And ever as the glass he tends,
    His hungry eyes of God beseech
That light of Grace He will bestow,
    Or grains of saving wisdom teach.

"Dear Christ," he cries, "perchance Thy feet
    Thou on this desert sand hast set;
Each grain Thy tear-drops have bedew'd—
    Thy agony of blood has wet.

"It knew Thee not—it knows not now
    The part that hour by hour it plays,
Marking the bounds of work and rest,
    Of steadfast prayer, and eager praise.

"And I!—what know I of the ends
    That we in Thy creation serve?
What boots the right when we are true,
    Or what the evil when we swerve?

"Of Thy good purpose in our lives
    (Or ignominious or sublime)
We dream as little as the sand
    Dreams that it marks the flight of time."

No more. On either globe, a star,
    The sea-green moonlight shimmers white ;
He sees it not, or sees as one
    Who gazes through some inner light.

But when the hour is done, and while
    There flickers down the last red grain,
He starts out of his dream, and turns
    The glass—and hark, his voice again !

" Dear Lord," he cries, " this desert sand
    Surely interprets Thee to-night !
For, while the missal glimmers dim,
    Its every sparkle glows with light.

" The secret mysteries of life
    My eyes are quickened to discern ;
Nor less, as thus I gaze and muse,
    The golden laws of duty learn.

"I mark that on its destined way
    The stream in ordered cadence goes;
Unhasting, but unceasing, still
    Without a sound it flows and flows.

"Whether thy solemn Word it mete,
    Or measure out a mortal stain;
It heeds not, questions not, but falls
    In rhythmic beauty, grain on grain.

"Let a saint's fingers grasp the glass,
    Or Judas hold it in his hand,
Nor one nor other may retard,
    Or quicken the insensate hand.

"'So go thou thine appointed way,'
    It seems to murmur to my soul;
'Achieve the purpose of a life
    Whereof thou seest not the whole.

"'Whatever gird thee round about
  Of seeming good or seeming ill,
Do thou thy duty; what befalls
  It is for God, not thee, to will.'"

The blue lips cease; but musing on
  He wrestles with the growing thought,
Until the shaven temples throb,
  There where a net the veins have wrought.

The night wears out, the moon goes down,
  The vine to fresher gusts is swung,
And lo! the squinting gargoyle thrusts
  From its stone mouth a stony tongue.

THE MISSAL.

Twine, O happy maiden,
  With thy tresses twine,
Tendrils flowing, roses glowing
  Red with red of wine.

Let thy radiant braidings
  Meet thy lover's eyes,
Like a golden page of olden
  Missal; flower-wise.

In a shining heaven
  Prankt with asphodel,
Angel of his love's evangel
  Ever shining dwell.

He will kneel, God praising
    For thy wonder-hair,—
"Lo, He painteth, lo, He scenteth,
    And He maketh fair!"

He will bend above thee
    Worshipping, I wis,
Almond-blossom brow and bosom—
    And thy mouth will kiss.

SANDS OF THE SEA.

Lapping as a dog will lap,
Crept the waves that mine and sap
Without violence, without shock,
Granite coast and isles of rock;

Crept into the placid bay,
Stealing up the sands that lay
Winnowed by the breeze, and white
With the bleaching of the light.

To the bay had wandered down
Idlers from the little town,
Summer-idlers, labour free,
Happy by the shining sea.

SANDS OF THE SEA.

Slowly to and fro they went,
Or, in dreamy musing, bent,
And the fancy and the thought
On the rippled sand they wrought.

There a boy with locks of light
Drew himself a famous kite,
That against the wind would sail,
Streaming prodigal of tail.

There a maiden, violet-eyed,
Drew her thought, and, drawing, sighed,—
At her feet a lover's face
Outlined in exceeding grace.

And a poet, lean and sad,
Hollow-eyed as he were mad,
Traced the rhymes that wrought his pain,
Throbbing pulses in his brain!

Nor the old man's shaking hand
Spared the whitely tempered sand,
Thousands, hundreds, tens, he drew,—
All his fortune at a view!

But as each thus traced apart
That which quicken'd brain or heart,
Up the wave insidious crept
And from sight the record swept,—

Cared not for the famous toy,
Cared not for the maiden's joy,
Swept away the poet's rhyme
And the fortune in its prime!

Whitely crisping on its way
Thing of weakness, thing of play
It was pitiless withal,—
Wave more cruel did not crawl.

This the poet musing saw,
And he thought,—" Whom nature's law
Would discern, has far to seek
For her gauge of Strong and Weak.

" Giant forces that fulfil
Fruitful issues of her will,
Lurk in least suspected guise,
Hard to fathom or surprise.

" She is gentlest in her might;
Softest airs and waves unite
And a subtle purpose gain,
Where the storm has raged in vain.

" And however seeming frail,
Seeming slight, she does not fail,
But with strength in weakness moves
In her own elected grooves;

"Shaping all things to her plan,
 Ever pitiless to man
 As to all beneath her sway,—
 His her mandates to obey.

"Power fruitlessly he craves;
 Deaf to kingliest voice her waves,
 And as vainly each withstands
 Death's advances on life's sands."

Musing thus within his breast
Long he linger'd with the rest,—
Till the rosy evening came
And the day went out in flame:

Till a breeze, as darkness grew,
Fresh from round the headland blew,
And the ocean's heart of light
Throbbed beneath the purple night.

TO EVA, WITH A SONG.

I BRING to you my song, my little song,
    So wan, so weak, its breath is but a sigh,
O, feed it with the music of your voice,
    And it will throb with life : it will not die.

Take it, and haply for its sake—or mine—
    Your heart may warm toward it by-and-bye,
May come to deem it sweet, to hold it dear,
    And loved and cherished so, it cannot die.

THE GRANGE WINDOW.

The bar of red in the amber west
    Burns to ashes, and all is grey,
Though a sickle-moon is glittering out
    Through the haze of the dying day.

There is no light from the sickle moon,
    And fast the pearly greys grow dead,
The trees grow black and the flowers dim,
    Till the beauty of all has fled.

And the passion-flowers that, moonlight-hued,
    Tangle and twine with starry grace
About a window they garland up—
    Even these will the night efface.

Already the wine-red curtains folds
　　Hide the room with their ruddy glow,
And gone is the face that whitely gazed
　　At the sunset an hour ago.

Gone ! ah, no ; there is streaming again
　　A shaft of light athwart the gloom,
The dew-wet laurels within it gleam
　　And the flowers returning bloom.

That face once more ! and a rosy hand
　　The silken damask holds apart,
And full in the light a woman stands
　　With a trouble of eye and heart.

Full in the softening light that makes
　　A glory round her like a saint,
There stands the form that is Art's despair
　　And a face that no words can paint.

She watches and waits for one who stays,
    For one beloved she looks in vain,
And the big black eyes are full of tears
    And the child mouth quivers with pain.

Passionful longing and not reproach
    Steals the blood from her rounded cheek,
And sadness born of the hungering heart
    That can suffer but cannot speak.

" The hours drag on, O love of my heart!
    Wearily on, and you are not here;
A hundred terrors oppress my brain
    I am sick to swooning with fear.

" It is not doubt, O life of my life!
    O truest, and fondest, and best;
But I am a woman, and womanly fears
    Rend and distract my breast."

So the white lips murmuring move,
  Yet the while with her wistful eyes
She gazes into the garden's gloom
  And up at the brightening skies.

The sickle moon has the gleam of gold
  In the deepening blue above,
She thinks " It shines not for me alone,
  It is shining on him I love."

But hark ! what echo the silence breaks,
  And what sound when all sound seemed dead?
Her cheek is fading from red to white
  And is flushing from white to red ;

And the big eyes glisten. Yet these alone
  Are the sounds which her ears await,—
A hasty footstep spurning the road
  And a hand on the garden gate.

ROSE SONG.

Sunny breadths of roses,
    Roses white and red,
Rosy bud and rose leaf
    From the blossom shed!
Goes my darling flying
    All the garden through,
Laughing she eludes me,
    Laughing I pursue.

Now to pluck the rose-bud,
    Now to pluck the rose,
(Hand a sweeter blossom)
    Stopping as she goes :

What but this contents her,
  Laughing in her flight?
Pelting with the red rose,
  Pelting with the white.

Roses round me flying,
  Roses in my hair,
I to snatch them trying,—
  Darling, have a care!
Lips are so like flowers,
  I might snatch at those
Redder than the rose leaves,
  Sweeter than the rose.

HOME AGAIN.

Home again! spared the perils of years,
    Spared of rough seas and rougher lands,
And I look in your eyes once, once again,
    Hear your voices and grasp your hands!

Not changed the least, least bit in the world!
    Not aged a day as it seems to me!
The same dear faces, the same dear home,—
    All the same as it used to be!

Ah! here is the garden! Here the limes
    Still in their sunset green and gold,
And the level lawn with the pattern in't
    Where the grass has been newly roll'd.

And here come the rabbits lumping along,—
   No! that's never the same white doe
With the pinky lops and the munching mouth;
   Yet 'tis like her as snow to snow.

And here's Nep in his old heraldic style,
   Erect, chain-tightening all he can,
With Topsy wagging that inch of tail,—
   What, you know me again, old man?

The pond where the lilies float and bloom!
   The gold fish in it just the same,
Too fat to stir in the cool,—yes, one
   Shoots, and gleams, and goes out like flame!

And still in the meadow, daisy-white,
   Its whistling flight the arrow wings,
And the fallen target's central " gold"
   Glitters—a planet with its rings!

And yonder's the tree with the giant's face,
    Sharp nose and chin against the blue,
And the wide elm-branches meeting, bear
    Our famous swing between the two.

No change! nay, it only seems last night
    I blurted back your fond good-byes,
As I heard the rain drip from the eaves
    And felt its moisture in my eyes.

Only last night that you throng'd the porch,
    Each choking words we could not say,
And poor little Jim's white face peep'd out,
    Dimly seen while I stole away.

Poor little Jim! in this happy hour
    His wee, white face our hearts recall,
And I miss a hand and a voice, and see
    The little crutch beside the wall.

So all life's sunshine is fleck'd with shade,
  So all delight is touch'd with pain,
So tears of sorrow and tears of joy
  Welcome the wanderer home again!

THE PAGE.

Like a missal, all ablaze
    With the gold and colours blended,
Shine the bright chivalric days
    In their hazy distance splendid.

Knights in long processions go,
    Tossing plumes and armour flashing,
Pennons interblending glow,
    Glaives are shining, falchions clashing.

Maidens lone in 'leagured towns
    Dreaming over minstrel praises,—
Yard-long hair and silken gowns
    (Sunny meadows prankt with daisies).

Lips that meeting lips bespeak,
    Side long glances, smiles ecstatic;
Flowers freshening in the cheek,
    Sighs distinctly aromatic.

Nobly born as passing fair,
    For though sweet are thicket roses,
Perfect blooms of the parterre,
    Only the parterre discloses.

Then at every maiden's side,
    Sworn companion of her leisure,
Moves Sir Page,—my lady's pride
    Pleasing torment, tiresome pleasure.

Clad in suit of iris hues,
    Hawk on wrist, with bells and jesses,
Eyes of liquid browns or blues,
    Maiden cheeks and maiden tresses.

Fond of joust and fond of brawl—
    Dagger out ere word is spoken—
Life of bower, and life of hall,
    Youth's free spirit all unbroken.

Singing to the twangling lute
    Minstrel ballad last in fashion,
Till the lips that should be mute
    Learn the parrot-lisp of passion.

Underneath the pleasaunce walls,
    (Ripe with nectarines and peaches),
Glad my Lady's damozels
    List the lesson that he teaches.

Eyes upon a blushing face,—
    Curls against a milky shoulder,—
Arm about a resting place
    Might dismay a lover bolder.

Of his heart and its despair,
    Vowing oft and oft protesting,
Till so much of love is there,
    Only half of it is jesting.

Happy Page, who thus can move
    In a round of bright enjoyment—
Happy to whom song and love
    Represent life's sole employment!

BARREN FAITH.

O, FRIEND, we nurse in vain a scholar-faith,
   Though one that with its husky logic feeds
   And satisfies our intellectual needs;
How should this move to good or guard from scaith?
Begot of schoolmen's subtleties alone
   It carries with it no awakening force,
   Life is not quickened by it in its course;
The head is ever cool; the heart a stone.
Such dead-seed faith is with no saving rife,
   It does not, cannot blossom into aught
   Of active goodness, is mere barren thought
That never can become a law of life.
Something the soul demands on which to thrive;
If it is saved, it must be saved "alive."

HARALD'S WOOING.

GLOOMY is Rother, gloomier none,
King of the Isles of the Setting Sun.

Word came to him "Thy daughter grieves,
Her cheeks are thinner than winter leaves."

Word came to him "Thy Thora is lorn,
For Harald the Jute her heart is torn."

With anger kindled his falchion-eye,
"Accursed live I, accursed die,

If ever by word or ever by sign
I welcome the Harald for son of mine!"

They bore the maiden the words he spake,
Never a tear from her eyelids brake;

From noon to night, and from night to noon,
She sat her as one that maketh to swoon.

For many a day her maidens said,
" She fareth her less alive than dead."

And every morn they hearkened her breath,—
Or lay she in sleep or lay she in death?

In the month of the leafing of trees
There came a ship from over the seas:

Its sides of gold were brighter than flame,
But none might tell of it whence it came.

Never a knight on its deck it bore,
But he who trod it was bent and hoar,

His wide robe wrought in many a fold
With dragons in jewels and cords of gold.

O, few were his words and passing strange,
"For ever from land to land I range

The sick to heal and the dead to raise :
And banish sorrow and end of days!"

To Rother the King the Sage they brought ;
"These, King, are the wonders he hath wrought!"

And he said, "My child is like to die :
Hath philtre or charm can love defy?"

"Yea, King," he answered, "bring thou to me
Thy daughter fair and this thing shall be."

"The maiden straight to thy vessel bring—
Must it be so?" "As thou sayest, King :

Nay, since to doubting thy heart is prone,
She comes not, coming not there alone!"

The ship's gold sides on the waves burn red,
Her foam-white sails to the winds are spread.

From the shore it speedeth, a bird of flight;
The King's fair daughter, in wild affright,

Cries to the seas and cries to the shore.
" Peace! if thou lovest me, Lady Thore!"

He has slipt the robe that fold on fold
Is wrought with dragons in gems and gold;

And quick to the reddened waters go
The drift-white locks and the beard of snow;

Ring-golden tresses and ruddy cheek
The grace and glory of youth bespeak—

And who upriseth from Thora's feet
But Harald the Jute, her lover meet:

Harald, who danger and hate defied,
With love-craft winning his winsome bride?

THE LETTER.

How daintily it lies on the crisp moss
There, in the hollow bole of the great elm,
Pure in its morning freshness! The white leaves,
With delicate enfoldment interwrought,
Close, flower-like, fold on fold; and, look, for seal
A dew-drop glistens! Blossom of the night!
Who comes to pluck it in the amber dawn?
Whose sleep was light for heart-throb, and who heard,
Deep in a dream, the bickering sparrows stir
And twitter in the ivy on her walls?

   The terrace marble gives not back her step,
So lithe of spring: the garden only hears

A silken creeping as she glimmers through
And out into the Chace, that stirs not yet,
But holds the mists in it, as eyes hold sleep.
Straight to the antler'd elm she glides, and waits,
Thinking, " It cannot be !" and yet again
" It cannot—cannot be !" then stoops, and thrusts
Her white arm, to the elbow, through the rift
Where the elm parts, and cries out joyously.
O happy, childlike cry ! O glad, bright eyes,
And tingling cheeks, and ear-lobes hotly stung !
Her heart in the wild tumult of its bliss
Speaks thus : it is so bless'd. The prize is found !
She grasps the flower of Love's own spring-time
 born !
It is her own, to fondle, to bedew
With happy tears, or press to those red lips
That will not part from it, but cling and cling.

And now let all be still. Let no dead leaf
Or hasty footstep scare. Alone—alone—

Secure from peering eye or curious ear,
She will feed love on love's ambrosia.
See how her flaming eyes devour the page!
Words had no worth, thoughts never glow'd till now,
Language was never music till this hour.
How sweet it is, how precious! Radiant bloom,—
She will suck out thy honey drop by drop,
Insatiate still: still loth to part with thee
To her soft bosom's keeping, though the Chace
Swim round her as she reads, and she is fain
To clutch at the wet leaves on the low boughs,
Fearing to swoon for utter ecstacy.

LOVE SONG.

I TOUCH the keys and wait,
    Watching the dreamful eyes
That hide their thoughts, as stars
    Hidden in bluest skies;
What choice will shape the swain
    Will soothe my heart ere long,
When song gives back to life
    The hours when life was song?

O, dreamful eyes that hide
    Their secret thought so well,
A burning cheek reveals,
    A silent lip can tell:

When youth will sing to youth
    What from its heart must throng?
Love it has ever sung,
    Love is its only song.

THE FAMOUS STORY.

The shadows of the little wood
    Closed round us in the burning noon,
The lucent shadows of the leaves,
    Yet tender with the green of June.

And there, while in a happy dream,
    We wandered inward from the sun,
Winding and turning at our will,
    The famous story was begun.

A story prodigal of love,
    Of youth, and beauty born of youth;
Of sorrow tempered by romance,
    And trial glorified by truth.

Long, long ago it all had chanced,—
   Or was it haply passing then?
It might be true of any time
   Since women were beloved of men.

I listened, yet I did not heed;
   A rippling voice was all I heard,
That, softly cadenced, had for me
   The music of a singing bird.

The tale went on, the voice I heard,
   Yet all that I recall is this,—
That earnest face, those dreamy eyes,
   The little mouth so sweet to kiss.

The tale went on, with many a pause,
   With frequent outbursts of delight,
As breaks and openings of the wood
   Its hidden beauties gave to sight.

A pheasant gleamed across our path,
    A squirrel shot a sudden turn,
And now the cuckoo sang, and now
    We waded coolest breadths of fern.

The little wood was long to cross;
    Its winding paths were hard to find;
And hours had fled ere we emerged,
    And left its pleasant gloom behind.

And then beside the rustic fence,
    Whence spread the meadows many a mile,
We linger'd idly hand in hand,—
    And still the tale went on the while.

The evening shadows lengthened out;
    The heavy rooks winged home to nest;
The little wood was fringed with light
    Against the fiercely flaming west.

The sun set in a fleecy haze,
    Sank flaming in a sea of gold,
The sky grew dark, the stars came out,
    And yet the story was not told!

A DREAM OF THE SEA.

The great cliffs crimson overhead,
    Hid in their purple glooms we go,
The waves break frothing at our feet
    In-running break with frothy snow ;
Here roam we, darling, where the rock
    Steeps down into the seething sea,
And dream that save the waste of night
    There is no world for thee and me.
Against the greening sunset gold
    Die out the crimson-purple bars,
The day is gone, the night is near,
    A day of flowers, a night of stars.

The meadow odours of the sea
    Rise as we stray with folded palms,
Glad in our world of winds and waves,
    Of rending storms and rosy calms;
To us the far is as the past,
    The gleamy headland's dying line
Is equal bound of time and space,—
    This heart-beat, is it thine or mine?
The last faint gleam of gold is gone,
    Black grow the crimson-purple bars;
Love glorified the day of flowers,
    Love sanctifies the night of stars.

THE LORELEI.

" Flows the Rhine as flowing wine,
  Bright in its unrest,
Sweet with odours of the vine;
  Heaven in its breast."

So the boatman Hugo sung,
  Long, aye, long ago,
While the Rock its shadow flung
  In the sunset glow.

At that fortalice, upraised
  From its purple base,
Suddenly the boatman gazed
  With a stricken face.

On its summit, wondrous fair,
    Shining angel-wise,
Sat a maid, with golden hair
    And beseeching eyes.

From a shoulder's rosy sphere
    All the robe that slid,
Ripple-bright and water-clear,
    Rather show'd than hid.

As her tresses sleeking through,
    Fingers pearly white,
Slowly went, the diamond dew
    Fell and broke in light.

But a cithern from her feet
    Lifted she ere long,
And its music, pulsing sweet,
    Fed a wondrous song.

And the boatman, drifting fast,
    Listen'd to his cost;
On the rocks before him cast!
    In the whirlpool lost!

Then the Lorelei's luring form
    Faded from the eye,
As a cloud fades, rosy warm,
    In a purple sky.

THE ASSASSIN.

BEHOLD one in a turret chamber, hung
    With picture-arras, where in conflict grim
    Titanic shapes, red-eyed and sprawl of limb
Counterfeit life, to gusts of midnight swung.
So tarry all amid the strange and rare
    Illusions that beguile us evermore,
    And lo! behind the arras is the door,
The treacherous portal of a secret stair!
And in the hour each deems him most alone,
    Seated secure from danger, he beholds
    A quick hand tear aside the arras folds,
And he is face to face with the Unknown;
With ready knife, or fingers stifling breath,
There falls upon him the assassin—Death!

THERESE.

Long weeks of weariness of brain,
    Long lapses of disordered dream,
And life is come to me again,
Delicious to the verge of pain,
    In utter ecstacy supreme.

Misdoubting all that I behold,
    I wander through the autumn days,
Strange splendour brightens hill and wold,
The woods are luminous with gold,
    The skies with amethyst ablaze.

And, like the spirit of the scene,
    So fair, I tremble as I gaze,
One wanders by my side, serene,
In perfect gracefulness of mien
    The darling of my heart—Thérèse.

And as the golden, glimmering eves
    Deepen about us, oft we gain
A trellised bower round which there weaves
A tangle of the wine-red leaves
    Wine-red as reddest wine may stain.

Then at my knee, with winning grace,
    She sits, her hair before me bright,
And, marble white, her earnest face
Gleams, till as darkness comes apace
    It glimmers to a spot of light.

And ever as we sit, she strives
    My languid fancy to beguile
With talk of great, of noble lives,
With tale or legend, that revives
    And cheers my drooping heart the while.

The bright creations of romance,
    The memories of vanished time,
Quicken resplendent in her glance;
But most my soul she will entrance
    With old-world witcheries of rhyme.

High aims and honorable deeds
    Shaped on her lips my heart will move
For sin and suffering she pleads;
But ever shuns the way that leads
    Toward the precipice of love!

That way the rosy pathways tend,
   Meandering ever as they go,
Where'er our devious course we wend
Love with each tender thonght will blend—
   Yet love's delights her lips forego.

For very pity she is lorn,
   The tear-drops glisten on her cheek ;
She pities and she does not scorn,
Yet out of pity love is born,
   And still of love she does not speak !

Strange ! yet, in sooth, far more I prize
   The love, a word of love dismays,
Straight to my hungering heart she flies,
For her alone it throbs or dies
   My darling, my delight—Thérèse !

MY LADY'S SECRET.

THAT night a drift-log from the sea there burn'd
   In the great chamber, and my Lady sat
With her white face and no-lips like a corse,—
   By the flames green and purple likest that!

Save near the hearth the chamber was all black,
   But the light play'd on her in diamond gleams
About her hair and bosom; and her robe
   Shone, stiff with gold, and rich with jewell'd seams.

Her wasted fingers from the miniver
   Of her long sleeves met in an interlace
About a silver crucifix: she prayed,
   Or prayed not,—none might read it in her face.

The carven chair of Lady Isobel,
    Her child, stood empty, but she heeded not;
Belike her thoughts were, with her heart, above,
    And all on this side heaven was forgot.

And yet she lifted eyes of sudden fear
    When the drawn arras show'd us as we crouch'd,
We servitors, and I gasp'd out the tale
    Of what had chanced, and what our looks avouch'd:

How, going with my fellows on our rounds
    To bolt and bar, as was our wont, that night,
We had beheld close to the postern door
    Our fair young mistress lying stark and white!

And whether she lay swooning, or lay dead,
    We knew not till we bore her up the stair,
All loth to touch with our coarse hands a form
    So pure, and, as it lay, so dainty fair.

Meekly my Lady listen'd, pressing hard
    Her hands, all gems, and mutter'd, "It is well;"
Then called her women, and rose up, and went
    Seeking where lay the Lady Isobel.

Who all as one that was too fair for death,
    Out of the swoon that held her captive, broke,
And mutter'd, "Leoline!" and yet again
    Cried, "Leoline!" and in that cry awoke.

Now other Leoline none knew save one,
    A fair tall stripling, full of clerkly guile,
And skilful on the lute, who oft had come
    And with his music sped the weary while.

But from that hour none saw him any more,
    None look'd upon his face nor heard his song;
And whispers gather'd, as the gathering wind,
    None knowing whence, of crime and secret wrong.

But naught of this my Lady heard, nor aught
    Came to the ears of hapless Isobel,
As in the castle's ever-deepening gloom
    They dwelt alone, contented thus to dwell.

Nor ever wander'd forth, though Autumn went
    Triumphal in a pageant through the land ;
But sat in the great chamber wide apart,
    Dumb, but with faces each might understand.

Till on a night, they sitting in this wise,
    The maiden rising, cried with stifled breath,
" You slew him—you !" and totter'd and fell down,
    All her white length, and there lay still in death !

This they who waited heard, and heard no more,
    But entering, saw my Lady's palsied guilt,
As she still sat, her cross upon the floor,
    Her broken rosary round about her spilt.

MY LADY'S SECRET.

Thus to her hapless grave went Isobel;
    And if my Lady wept her, who may know?
Or if guilt rankled 'neath the gold brocade,
    And diamonds palsy-tremulous in glow?

She took her secret with her, and the tomb
    Became—when solitary years had fled—
A casket for her dust, her gems, and *that*
    Shut close until the waking of the dead.

A SUMMER DREAM.

Only a summer dream,
    Sport of an idle day,
A meadow range, a word beside the stream,
    A parting and—away!

Only a dream of Love,
    Of heart inclined to heart—
As clouds that in the blue of heaven meet,
    As white clouds cling and part.

We dream'd and we awoke;
    No more! But ah, for dreams
Engender'd of the subtle light of Love,
    Bright with its iris gleams!

Shadows of leaf and bird
    Fall on the meadow grass ;
But over it the shadow that I love
    Never again shall pass.

The summer voices blend
    In music as of yore,
But from the melody has dropt a note :
    There will be song no more.

The glory and the wealth
    Of Nature all things share,
But in my heart is no responsive throb
    That tells me it is fair.

Back on the sunny dream
    I turn an aching gaze,
But the clear splendour of its glory throws
    A shadow on my days.

THE FLIGHT FOR LIFE.

O, HIDEOUS leagues of straining woods,
    Straining back from the sea;
O, woods of pine, and nothing but pine,—
    Will they never have end for me?

The ceaseless line of the red, red pine
    My very brain it sears;
And the roar of trees, like surging seas,
    Is it ever to haunt my ears?

Let me remember it all. 'Twas late—
    The burning end of day;
The trees were all in a golden glow,
    As with flame they would burn away.

THE FLIGHT FOR LIFE.

The joyful news to our clearing came,
    Came as the sun went down :
A ship from England at anchor lay
    In the bay of the nearest town.

In that good ship my Alice had come—
    Alice, my dainty queen !
Sweet Alice, my own, my own so near—
    There was only the wood between !

Now, three days' journey we counted that,
    The days and nights were three ;
But for thirty days and thirty nights
    I had journeyed my love to see.

Before an hour to the night had gone,
    Into the wood I went ;
The pine-tops yet were bright in the light,
    Though below it was all but spent.

'The moon at ten and the dawn at four!'
    For this I offered praise;
Though I knew the wood on the hither side,
    Knew each of its tortuous ways.

The moon rose redder than any sun,
    Through the straight pines it rose;
But glittered on keener eyes than mine,
    On the eyes of deadliest foes!

To sudden peril my heart awoke—
    And yet it did not quail;
I had skirted Indians in their camp,
    And the fiends were upon my trail!

Three stealthy Snakes were upon my track,
    Supple and dusk and dread;
A thought of Alice, a prayer to God,
    And like wind on my course I sped.

Only in flight, in weariest flight,
   Could I my safety find;
But fast or slow, howe'er I might go,
   They followed me close behind.

The night wore out and the moon went down,
   The sun rose in the sky;
But on and on came the stealthy foes,
   Who had made it my doom to die.

With two to follow and one to sleep,
   They tracked me through the night;
But one could follow and two could sleep,
   In the day's increasing light.

So all day under the burning sky,
   All night beneath the stars;
And on, when the moon through ranging pines
   Gleamed white as through prison-bars.

With some to follow and some to halt,
    Their course they well might keep;
But I—O God, for a little rest,
    For a moment of blessed sleep!

Lost in the heart of the hideous wood,
    My desperate way I kept;
For why? They would take me if I stayed,
    And murder me if I slept.

But brain will yield and body will drop;
    And next when sunset came,
I shrieked delirious at the light,
    For I fancied the wood on flame!

I shrieked, I reeled; then venomous eyes
    And dusky shapes were there;
And I felt the touch of gleaming steel,
    And a hand in my twisted hair.

A cry, a struggle, and down I sank;
    But sank not down alone,—
A shot had entered the Indian's heart,
    And his body bore down my own!

Yet an Indian gun that shot had fired—
    Most timely, Heaven knows!
For I had chanced on a friendly tribe,
    Who were watching my stealthy foes.

And they who fired had kindliest hearts:
    They gave me nursing care;
And when that my brain knew aught again,
    Lo, my Alice, my own, was there!

Amid their dusky forms she stood
    Fair to my feeble sight,
As a shining angel God had sent
    In a halo of blinding light.

Dear Alice ! But O, the straining woods,
    Straining back from the sea ;
The woods of pine, and nothing but pine,
    They have never an end for me.

The ceaseless line of the red, red pine
    My brain to madness sears ;
And the roar of trees, like surging seas,
    Is the horror that fills my ears.

VALLEY MEMORIES.

WAKING I dream, and dreaming see
    A valley in the sunset glow,
With ranging Alps that through the haze
    Thrust peaks of snow.

A blinding glare is in my eyes;
    Yet, far below, I see again,
Where, golden under burning skies,
    Outsweeps the plain.

All freshly fair and bright the scene;
    But looming vast before me still
The Alps gigantic grow, and all
    The picture fill.

Their spell once more is on my heart,
    Their grandeurs satisfy the soul ;
Naught else in life or space has part—
    They make the whole.

They wrap the heavens round their forms,
    Arrest the clouds upon their march,
And into gleaming ruins break
    The rainbow's arch.

From the deep valley's purpling gloom
    Ever their summits rise sublime,
Bright with the sunsets of the world
    Since Time was Time.

CANONBURY PARK, MAY 30TH.

THAT day the shining aspens swayed
   With music as of hidden seas,
   The netted shadows of the trees
Fleck'd all the lawn with restless shade;
The branching pear pavilioned us,
   Its gold the light laburnum shed,
   Danæ was wooed afresh, we said,
And summer dreamt of Pactolus.
The affluent sweetness of the day
   Quickened the pulses of delight,
   Wit challenged laughter in its flight,
As we were happy we were gay,
And time to sweeter music moved
With those we prized and those we loved.

THE TROOPER'S DEFENCE.

Do I plead guilty to it? Yea, I do;
    For I have never lied, and shall not now;
But give me a dog's leave to say a word
    Touching what happened, and the why and how.

The night-guard went their rounds that night at one;
    My post was in the lower dungeon range,
Down level with the moat, all slime and ooze
    And damp; but there, 'tis fit we change and change,

We sentinels.   Besides, 'twas in a sort
   The place of honour, or of trust, we'll say ;
For in the cell there with the mortised door
   The young boy-lord, guilty of treason, lay.

Well, with my partisan I'd tramped an hour
   Down in the dark there—just a lantern hung
By the wet wall—when close at hand I heard
   My own name spoken by a woman's tongue.

My hair was like to lift my morion up,
   For the keep's haunted ; but I turned, to see
A woman like a ghost—face white, all white,
   Ready to drop, and not a yard from me.

How she had come there God in heaven knows.
   However, long before my tongue I'd found,
She tore out of her hair the white pearls, big
   As pigeon's eggs, then dropt upon the ground.

"One word!" she said, "only one word with him;
　　He dies to-morrow! See, my pearls I give,
My bracelets too"—she slipt them from her arms—
　　"One word, and I will bless you while I live!

"Your face is stern. O, but one word, one word!"
　　With my big hand I set her on her feet;
But she clung to me, would not be thrust off,
　　Still pleading in a bird's voice, soft and sweet.

"Only one word with him!" that was her plea;
　　One word; he would be dead at break of day!
She wept till all her pretty face was wet,
　　And my heart melted: yea, she had her way.

They spake together. Did I hear? Not I;
　　Best ask me if I took her bribes. Well, there,
You know the rest—know how yon Judas-spy,
　　　Yon starveling cur, crawled down the winding stair;

And how he caught the bird fast in the cage,
    And made report of me with eager breath
For breach of duty. Right ; it was a breach,
    And that means, in our soldier-fashion, death !

Well, I can face it : only give me leave
    To slit the weasand of yon craven hound,
Yon Judas-spy there, and I'd fall content,
    Aye, as I'd fall to sleep upon the ground.

ALLEGORY.

As through his life's dark night the Prophet went,
    Ever the stars shone brightly overhead,
And, gazing on the fretted firmament,
    " These are God's flaming altar-fires " he said ;
" But earth is dark and cold, and renders not
    From her hard bosom homage to His name.
God of his stars is glorified : forgot
    Alone of man who should His praise proclaim !"
Then of his best he took and straightway heaped
    Beside the way an altar and gave fire,
And high the joyous flames fantastic leaped—
    " Lo ! they put out the stars !" he cried, and higher

Heaped up the precious fuel; yet would bound
    And sink the flames wherewith the clouds grew
        red :
Ever they dropped, and darkness closing round
    Sucked out their life. Yet gazing undismayed,
" It shall not die for lack of aught " he cried,
    " Though of my life a sacrifice be made."
But though the altar with himself he fed,
    The fire went out, and still the stars shone overhead.

THE 'PRENTICE HOLIDAY.

LONDON, JANUARY 30, 1661.

INTO a sky as blue as May
We threw our 'prentice caps that day,
And all was bright as if the Spring
Had come to see that wondrous thing,
  The white rose bloom again!

Upon a loyal deed intent
Down to the minster first we went,
Out of his grave old Noll we drew,
And Ireton seized, and Bradshaw too,
  The white rose blooms again!

THE 'PRENTICE HOLIDAY.

To Tyburn straight we haled the three,
And strung them high on Tyburn tree,
Our voices rising clear and strong:
A thousand throats, a single song,
   " The white rose blooms again!"

One in a cloth of green was wrapped,
A murray serge one overlapped,
And one was in his winding sheet—
It hung a yard below his feet.
   The white rose blooms again!

They hung with faces white and spare,
And eyes that seemed to blink the glare;
Yet so like life, it troubled some
To think " If Noll to life could come!"
   The white rose blooms again!

A vintner pointed to the tree
And cried, " A famous trinity ;
None greater and none less in evil,
But equal—satan, fiend, and devil!"
   The white rose blooms again !

" And here, again," another cried,
" Christ with two thieves was crucified ;
Now tell us, crop ears, by your leaves,
Which is the Christ, which are the thieves?"
   The white rose blooms again !

One held a flagon in the light,
And cried, " Old Noll, thy nose is white,
Here is the drink thou lovest most,
Drink ! an thou choke not with the toast."
   " The white rose blooms again !"

Long in the burning sun they hung,
Long in the breeze they swayed and swung;
It was the headsman lowered the dead,
From every corse he smote its head.
   The white rose blooms again!

Aloft on pikes the heads they bore,
Then up there went a parlous roar,
And one cried, " Noll, thou'dst kings defy,
But never yet held head so high :
   The white rose blooms again!"

By this the sun drew near the west;
We wended homeward with the rest,
But when the day to darkness turned
At Temple Bar a bonfire burned :
   The white rose blooms again!

And so the martyr's day we kept,

Long may his cruel end be wept,

And England cry " Long live the King!"

And long live we to shout and sing—

    " The white rose blooms again!"

A LOST LOVE.

I see her as I met her in the hour
    When love's first impulse quickened in her breast,
Warm as the roseate flushes of the dawn,
    A fresh delight that knew not of unrest.

In the resplendent blossom of her youth
    She comes before me, prodigal of grace,
And in the calm of summer hours again
    My heart grows amorous of her peerless face.

Once more her winning eyes look into mine,
    Her rosy hands again are mine to hold,
And round her, bright as from a fountain, flow
    Her rippling tresses luminous with gold.

In memory we wander side by side,
    Our hearts responsive and our shadows one :
And still upon my lips the word unsaid,
    That shaping oft as oft they quivering shun.

Ever my heart is full ; my lips are mute
    Till on a day when all the world is fair,
The birds sing and the blossoms breathe of love,
    And I my love have murmured unaware.

And through her crimson blushes she replies
    In whispers—softest music every tone—
Owning her love, and trembling as she owns
    Her passion has interpreted my own.

That moment I recall as one recalls
    All day the sweetness of a waking dream :
But Time can mar the bliss that Time can make,
    And darkest shadows snare the sunniest gleam.

As there had come an hour that saw us meet,
    So in the end an hour of parting came :
Our sudden love had no enduring heat,
    And perished, haply, as too fierce of flame.

We are of those who pace opposing shores,
    And, pondering what is, what might have been,—
Stretch out their craving hands that may not meet,
    For Time, a ruthless ocean, flows between !

A. T. M.

ALL the abounding beauty of her form,
The mellowing sweetness of her quickening mind,
The glorious issue of a heart of love,—
All, all transformed at thy grim presence,—
    Death!

No watched decay and no denoted change;
No fading cheek, no lustre-lacking eye;
Nor any laughter wanting to our mirth!
And thy chill cry rings on our sleeping ears—
    O Death!

Coiled at our feet in sweet obedient love
Caught to our hearts, her failings all forgot,
A tyrant in her beauty! now so still:
Lying so mute, so patient in thy thrall,—
    Terrible Death!

E'en now, the drowsy hush of summer leaves
A slumbrous calm about her fitly keeps:
We who so loved her leave her—for awhile;
Leave her to thy long cherishing, O Death;
    O gentle Death!

THE SPECTRE.

They saw a Spectre in the setting sun,
    Those eyes of a great nation, westward turned,
Beheld it vast and splendrous, as with light,
    As with white light, it burned.

"Lo! here," they cried, "is Glory, born of God,
    Inspiring noble aims and shining deeds;
What should we do but listen to its voice,
    And follow as it leads?

"Ignoble are the arts and toils of Peace,
    Her hoarded fruits and harvests ripely stored:
The sickle for the masters of the world
    Is the man-reaping sword!"

Forth in their might they poured, to meet a foe
    Worthy their prowess, worthy their defeat ;
With clouds of hovering hosts the land was black—
    They met as oceans meet.

Two seas that crashing in tumultuous might,
    With hurling waves, and each to each a shore,
Whereon live men were broken in the shock,
    And whelmed in spraying gore.

And only with the dusk the tide went out,
    And left the dead and those who could not die,
To the shrill winds that mocked them, and the rains
    Of a low, wailing sky.

And the great winds were charged with blasphemies,
    The taint of blood was in the falling rain
That could not quench the burning wounds of men
    Grown envious of the slain.

And, lo! the Spectre in the glimmering dawn
  Stood robed in blood, as on the overnight,
In ever-flowing blood that, in the blaze
  Of light, had glistened light.

THE WINDING OF THE SKEIN.

THE orchard trees are white with snow
    As they were white with bloom,
Foam-white, and like a sea, beneath
    The window of the room;
And fitfully the April sun
    Strove with the April rain,
But brightest glinted out to see
    The winding of the skein.

We were two sisters, Maud and I,
    And were content to dwell
In the old house among the trees
    Our mother loved so well;

Our friends were few, and other friends
    We never sought to gain;
The chief was he whose name recals
    The winding of the skein.

Our artist neighbour, Clement, loved
    The orchard like a boy,
Its blossom roof, its mossy boughs
    Made half his summer joy,
And like a brother in our hearts
    He grew in time to reign,
And it was Maud and he who wrought
    The winding of the skein.

I marked them often, saw and read
    The wonder on his face,
And how his artist eye approved
    Her beauty, and the grace

THE WINDING OF THE SKEIN.

That kindled an admiring love
    He struggled to restrain,
Until the day she bade him help
    The winding of the skein.

Ring after ring the golden floss
    About his fingers roll'd;
He thought, " Her hair is brighter yet,
    It has the truer gold."
I read this in the eyes that strove
    To turn from her in vain,
And loathed my raven tresses through
    The winding of the skein.

Round after round they wound before
    The task was wholly done,
And if their fingers touched, the blood
    Straight to his cheek would run;

And if the knotted silk she chid,
    Her voice through every vein
Went with a thrill of joy throughout
    The winding of the skein.

Round after round until the end,
    And when the end was there,
He knew it not, but sat with hands
    Stretch'd in the empty air ;
The ringing of her merry laugh
    Startled his dreaming brain,
And then he knew his heart ensnared
    In winding of the skein.

Beneath the apple-blooms that day
    And many a day they strayed,
I saw them through a mist of tears,
    While hard for death I prayed,

And like those blossoms still, these snows
    Benumb my heart with pain ;
But Maud knows not why I recall
    The winding of the skein.

IN A FRIEND'S POETICAL WORKS.

To this enchanted wood I came, and saw
    Where its star-centre glimmer'd, ever bright,
Through branches infinite. And as I stray'd,
    Plucking a blossom, colour-pure as light,
Or leaf, a flow'r in brightness—lo ! there peep'd
    Through screening leaves the blue eyes of a Fay,
Which straight, " in small frock, as a snowdrop white,"
    Came forth, and I beheld her—Baby May !
She to the wood's heart pointed, and I, glad
    To utter gladness, follow'd, losing soon
All sense but of the wonder that I had,
    And a great joy of freshness. This, a tune

Of sweetest music, helped : a pleasant strain
   That, flowing as we onward moved, seem'd born
Of the green leaves, or the soft winds, or came
   Of waters, or the surge of ripen'd corn ;
And yet not so, though all in it had part,
   'Twas but the Poet singing, glad of heart.

THE LOST.

On the hills the wind was fierce,
    All night long they heard it blow;
But the little town lay calm,
    Whitening with the falling snow.

From her sleep the pastor's wife
    Started up in sore affright:
"Listen, husband: some one cries!"
    "Wife, the winds are loud to-night."

"'Twas our child, our Glinka's voice;
    Twice again I heard her cry!"
"Rest thee, wife; the night is wild,
    And the winds are raging high."

THE LOST.

With the dawn the wind went down,
    Calm above as calm below,
And the little town lay still
    With the stillness of the snow.

But while yet the morn was gray,
    Cries the deadly silence broke:
Clam'rous knocking fill'd the house;
    Sick of heart the mother woke.

To the casement huddled straight:
    Saw where, through the little street,
Men her child, her Glinka, bore,
    Bending low at head and feet.

" Mistress, see; we bring thy child,
    Frozen by the cruel night!"
But she heeded not nor spoke;
    She had neither voice nor sight.

In the chamber lay the dead ;
    Bitter words the pastor spake :
"He the wretch who lured her forth,
    God forget and man forsake !"

Heeding not and hearing naught,
    Rocked the mother to and fro :
"Cruel ! cruel ! Thrice she cried ;
    And I heard and did not go !"

THE DEAD OF THE YEAR.

Through the dead winter days I go,
Under cloud skies, that, hanging low,
Deaden the colour and the light;
The noonday sun is cold and white,
And frequent falls on hill and plain
A mist as heavy as a rain.

There is no warmth in Nature's breast,
No beauty glorifies her rest;
No sunrise and no sunset glow,
The flowers have perished long ago;
And all the scene is tempered down
To gray of gray and brown of brown.

From the gaunt trees else wholly bare
A wet leaf shudders here and there,
Or swirling drops, while all the ground
Is with a sodden drift embrowned;
Not crisp nor rustling to the tread,
The music of the leaves is dead.

The year is dead, and ah, my heart
Has in its torpor place and part;
Nor mourns the autumn's golden prime,
Ever a bright and treacherous time;
That cheated it with light and bloom,
And left it empty as the tomb.

Still I recall the splendrous glow
Of autumn—when the sun was low;
In kindled heavens quick with flame,
Through the red woods a goddess came,
A halo in her amber hair,
And I looked on in mute despair.

As from a missal's burnished skies
The angels look, she looked with eyes
Whose gaze wrought on me like a spell;
O'er summer heavens her eyelids fell,
And for her face—the flush and pride,
Of ripening autumn it outvied.

There was no line, no dainty curve.
That did not to perfection serve
In that rare form so subtly fair,
It lent a splendour to the air;
And seemed, to eyes that looked and loved,
To make the light through which it moved.

My heart awoke from out its sleep,
A fiery passion, pure and deep
As a man's heart may know, I knew;
I saw her fair, I held her true,
And prayed that love my life might bless
And kindle into happiness.

I held her true, I saw her fair,
No warning bade my heart beware,
The cruel lips that falsely smiled,
The words that wantonly beguiled;
I heeded not; the siren strain
Had ravished ear, and heart, and brain.

She loved or loved not, who might say?
When she bent o'er me as I lay
Lapp'd on that spicery, her breast,
She spoke in earnest, spoke in jest,
I did not question which. In youth,
Love's only other name is truth.

As one into his eyes should press,
Charm'd juice of love-in-idleness;
So eyes and heart a rapture swathed,
In bliss my lightened being bathed,
Till all too late I grew to know
My seeming joy my bitterest woe.

This simple truth was hard to learn,
They are not harshest lips that spurn,
They are not bitterest tears that fall,
Above the dead; worst, worst of all,
Life's direst anguish 'tis to prove
The loved unworthy of the love!

The truth came to me ere the dyes
Of autumn faded, ere its skies
Were gray with ashes of the pyres
Of its dead days : the sunset fires
Kindled the red woods as of yore,
My heart they kindle nevermore!

I cannot doubt of this, as bent
And crushed and broken, yet content,
In a dull wondering sort I go,
This is the uttermost of woe ;
And see, life's struggle wholly past,
Winter is welcome at the last.

For now low skies and stricken trees
Are all my comfort, all my ease,
In the dull pauses of my grief
The dead year comes to my relief;
It is an echo to my fate,
Since it and I are desolate.

DURING THE TERROR.

Ah, horror of blinding snow,
Red in the fiery glow;
But cold, so cold in the light!
We shudder'd that awful night—
Shudder'd and bitterly cried,
Though the fire we sat beside
Was of homesteads flaming high
Under the pitiless sky.

Placidly stood, that morn,
The homes where we were born—
We and our children, gay
In the sun of the winter day;

Deep in our household cares,
The world and the world's affairs
Troubled us not, though afar
Roll'd the blood-foaming billows of war.

Ah, pleasantly fell the snow,
Bright in the sunlight glow;
And the little ones, mad with fun,
Were clapping their hands, when one
Came spurring, fiery and fleet,
Up the heart of the little street,
With tidings of horror and fear,—
" They are here !—the enemy !—here !"

There ! And only the ridge
Of barren down and the bridge
To stay them ! Ere the sun
Went down their worst was done;

Our slain ones made the road
O'er which they tramp'd, and the goad
That drove us forth as they came,
Giving our homes to flame.

What had we done, dear Lord,
What that by fire and sword
We should for sin atone?
All things to Thee are known;
   And thou dost know
Wherefore this scathe, and flood
Of our sons' blood,
   And, out of heaven, the cruel, cruel snow.

BLUE EYES FOR TRUTH.

The ivy over-shines the wall,
    Her purple poison berries shed;
Ash-clusters blacken to their fall:
    The year is dead!

A fleck of amber, in the cloud
    That swathes the east, is dawn and light
And day, that mist and gloom enshroud,
    Makes welcome night.

As one who, seeing life depart,
    Ponders the wonder of our lives,
So, at the dead year's feet, my heart
    Strange thought revives.

I think of one, a blossom set
    Shining amid the snows of years;
Sweet in remembrance, in regret,
    Even in tears.

I see the bright rose of her face
    Flushed with the tender flush of youth,
And murmur, amorous of its grace,
    " Blue eyes for truth."

Blue eyes—the summer sky less blue—
    They were my rapture, my despair;
I knew them bright, and felt them true,
    Blue eyes that were!

Again I watch the cloud that lends
    The future all its rainbow dyes;
Again its veil the Phantom rends
    And rapture flies.

The anguish of each winter day
    Comes back into my heart anew ;
The charms death could not steal away
    Once more I view.

And in the wailing of the winds,
    The moan of branches swaying bare,
Again my soul re-echoed finds
    Its own despair.

The ivy over-shines the wall,
    The berries of the ash are shed ;
Under the holly's coronal
    The year lies dead !

SONG OF AGE.

When our feet were as feet of the dancer
    And the tones of our voices as song,
When the light was too fleeting for pleasure
    And the darkness for slumber too long,
We were glad and rejoiced in our being ;
    Our hearts were exultant in praise
For the rapture of loving and living
    And the infinite joy of our days.

Now the fervour of life has departed,
    We have emptied the gourds of delight,
We complain of the night " it is weary !"
    And we cry of the day " it is night !"

We are guests who have risen for going,
    And our hearts only quicken with praise,
For the languor that cometh of living
    And the torpor with ending of days.

BESIDE THE BROOK.

Brook that winding flowest
    Ever night and day,
Rippling as thou goest
    On thy shining way,
        In thy onward wending,
        Say, have all things ending,
Do the stars abide not, nor the flowers stay?

To thy beauty clinging
    All things meet and fair,
Of their sweetness bringing
    In thy being share,

Morns their freshness render,
Eves their rosy splendour,
But dost thou remember that their glories were?

When at noon thou shinest,
Sheathed in flaming gold,
Art thou gay, or pinest
'Neath the moonlight cold?
Do white willows sadden,
Blooming sedges gladden,
Or joyest when their plumage painted birds unfold?

Dream'st thou in thy gliding
Of a form of light,
That awhile abiding
Made thy waters bright,
Then with sudden spurning
Of love's eager yearning
Fled, and in its fleeing gave the world to-night?

Nay, as on thou farest,
As thy ripples sing,
Of her scorn thou sharest,
Nought remembering;
Speeding, only speeding,
Cold and all unheeding,
As she whose light a shadow o'er my life doth fling.

THE BALLAD OF THREE.

Three woke up in the quiet night
    Under the shining moon
From dreams of that which was to be
    Too soon, God knows, too soon.

One in a village of the wold,
    Tenderly nested, woke,
The very fulness of her joy
    The woof of slumber broke.

The tangled tresses from her face
    Her hand impatient swept,
Her cheek burned in the dark for joy:
    For joy she laughed and wept.

In pulsing raptures of delight
    All broad awake she lay,
The church vane kindled rosy gold,—
    It was her wedding day.

Deep in his castle's heart of gloom,
    Dull in the dawning gleam,
One started, shrieking from his sleep,
    As stricken in a dream.

And, rising fierce, he saw the stars
    Die out into the dawn,
As spots that fade into the gray
    Upon the dappled fawn.

And "O thou Mary—mother dear!"
    And "O thou Christ!" he said,
"Better this maid went to her grave
    Than to our marriage bed."

Out of the porch beside the church,
    Where crouched in gloom he lay,
One sprang with cries and cursed the stars
    And cursed the dawning day.

He drew a broad knife from his belt,
    Its edge was keen and true,
But on a stone that hid the dead
    He sharpened it anew.

And thrice across his thumb-nail wet
    The biting edge he tried :
" Once for my lord ! and once for me !
    And once for her his bride !"

So they three in the quiet night,
    They three beneath the moon,
Thought of the thing that was to be
    Too soon, God knows, too soon !

HOLLY TIME.

THE wood is barren as the wold
   The leaves have rusted long ago,
The flowers have perished of the cold,
Not even the hot marigold
   Offers her bosom to the snow
         In holly time.

The winds rend out the empty nest,
   The robin shivers in his song,
There is no warmth in Nature's breast,
Faint gleams of brightness at the best
   The glory of the year prolong
         In holly time.

Yet sweet as days when skies are blue
   And cherries redden on the wall :
When blossoms, fed with sun and dew,
Their beauty silently renew,
   Yea, sweeter, more desired of all
      Is holly time.

For now, as if the Incarnate Word
   Walked it again, the sterile earth
Rememb'ring the glad tidings heard
Of angels, to its heart is stirred
   With promptings of renewing birth
      This holly time.

Joy in life's pulses throbs and burns,
   The hours, star-crested, sweep along,
Shedding delight from brimming urns,
Youth to the heart of age returns,
   And fans the ashen brands of song
      In holly time.

The sacred hearths whence yule flames rise
　　Are altars whereon, each apart,
The households offer sacrifice
Out of the tender sanctities
　　And superstitions of the heart
　　　　　　In holly time.

Thus do celestial glimpses bless
　　The stricken world, as though its woes,
Its sins, its sorrows fathomless
Had ending, and the wilderness
　　Began to blossom as the rose
　　　　　　In holly time.

THE HOLLY'S TEACHING.

RUSTED are the golden leaves,
    Gone the blossoms trooping,
Gone the sparrows from the eaves,
    Rooks from elm-tops swooping:
Gleamy morns bring gloomy days,
    To lurid sunsets tending;
Snow-drifts whiten woods and ways,—
    So the year is ending.

But though winds despoil, and snows
    Hill and hollow deaden,
Wide the beacon Holly glows,
    Bright its berries redden;

Clear as with outspoken word
Hopeful comfort lending :
" Though the years die, hath the Lord
Of the dead years ending ?"

THE END.

ERRATUM.

In page 113, line 6, *for* " swain," *read* " strain."

TEN MILES FROM TOWN.

BY THE SAME AUTHOR.

CRITICAL NOTICES.

"A genial, picturesque, thoughtful book."—*Athenæum*.

"Pure poetry of a very tender and sweet order."—*Illustrated London News*.

"Full of tenderness and thoughtful grace."—*Bookseller*.

"They have the real ring by which we tell that poetic coin is not spurious."—*Standard*.

"Full of merit of a high order and promise of yet higher."—*Fun*.

"For colour, artistic flow, and sprightly elegance, these poems are very remarkable. . . . . A poet so thoughtful, so musical, and so picturesque, ought at once to gain the public ear."—*Public Opinion*.

"Sweet and gentle poetry."—*Christian World*.

"There is reason as well as rhyme in them, and the true genius of the poet declares itself in the changing metres."—*Nonconformist*.

"In all senses it is a choice, agreeable, and desirable possession."—*Sunday Times*.

"C'est donc avec le plus grand plaisir que nous saluons l'apparition du livre de M. Sawyer, un de ces ouvrages bien pensés et bien ecrit, où la poesie est simple et naturelle sans être terre à terre."—*L'International*.

"Mr. Sawyer does unquestionably write real poetry. 'Nymph and Satyr' might have been written by Heine."—*Illustrated Times*.

"Contains infinitely more poetry than volumes heralded by all preluding trumpets and announcements."—*Eclectic Review*.

"The author of this little book has strung together a necklace of poetic pearls among which it is difficult to choose the most valuable. The more the book is read the more it will be appreciated by all lovers of true poetry."—*Weekly Times*.

www.ingramcontent.com/pod-product-compliance
Lightning Source LLC
Chambersburg PA
CBHW021731220426
43662CB00008B/797